Make Money
Wood Burning

FOR LESS THAN $20!

Table of Contents

"Wood is universally beautiful to man. It is the most humanly intimate of all materials."

~ Frank Lloyd Wright

"Everyone Loves Wood!"

~ Lisa Fasulo

Everybody likes wood... and extra cash in your pocket.

The smell of wood burning is an instant stress reliever; the aroma is reminiscent of campfires, barbecues, and cozy winter fireplaces. People really love and admire wood burned designs. I'm not even sure they know why they are so captivated by decorated wood items, but I believe it's because it reminds them of all those warm and fuzzy memories of cozy fires and family BBQ's that they are channeling.

Wood is so completely satisfying to all our senses while touting a million different uses. We cook with it, build with it, and use it to keep us warm, among many other things! Wood is a common ingredient in most of our basic human needs.

Most importantly, wood has been serving mankind as an infallible income stream since the beginning of time... and that still holds true today!

How is wood going to serve YOU?

Allow me to show you how you can make money, at home, in your spare time, using one of the greatest resources in our history: wood.

So let's jump in and talk about how we can get YOUR wood burning business started for less than $20!!!

Chapter 1: Why Listen To Me?

I'm a serial entrepreneur whose motto has always been "lean and mean." My passion is starting up cottage businesses with little-to-no money. I like start-ups that have almost zero overhead because I believe it's the best way to give yourself a leg-up towards profitability. Plus, I hate failure so "lean and mean" works because it practically guarantees my success (I have to add that I'm always willing to do the footwork it takes to succeed).

Since the age of 13, I have earned money from arts and crafts projects I have created and sold. I started with hand painted wicker baskets which morphed into hand painted clothing. The hand painted clothing business was launched during my college years and ran successfully for 22 more years until I became too bored of painting T-shirts and sweatshirts.

I enjoyed consistent income in the high 5 figures for decades. There is always money in craft fairs.

From Canvas to Skin

Next up was tattooing. Permanent painting/drawing on skin. I obviously was comfortable with my art skills but didn't know how to break into the skin art business. As a seasoned DIY'er I imagined I could learn this trade easily. I was wrong. No one wanted to teach me and other artists wanted to keep their knowledge a secret. In the spirit of stubbornness, I didn't give up. I had many friends and fam that donated their skin to my education and I was eternally grateful. With each tattoo, my proficiency increased. Fast forward a few years: I created my own international tattoo school. I formed a bodyart school with a 2-week curriculum.

I created the kind of program that I would have appreciated attending. This business consistently brought me into the high 6 figures. Several years later, I happily sold the business to a competitor for a really, really good profit.

Along the way, I built up and sold a paint n' sip studio and a custom tattoo needle manufacturing company. These business life milestones of mine have proved to me, over and over again, that there is an amazing untapped potential of business opportunities in the arts and crafts field.

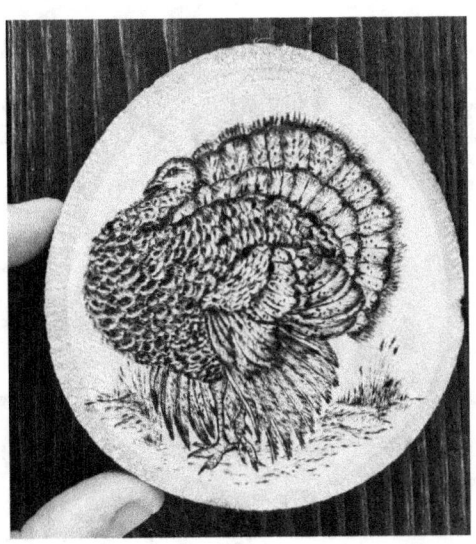

Enter Handmade Goods

Today, the business world has broadened into a global market and China is an ever-present supplier of underpriced goods. Marketplaces are flooded with mass-produced merchandise. But what can't be mass-produced as easily?

Hand-made goods.

The United States enjoys an over-abundance of wood, unlike China, and I have discovered wood as a new medium that interests me. I am intrigued with the calming effects it has, especially now when times today are fraught with anxiety and uncertainty.

Several years ago, I purchased a mobile bar trailer from China. The photos advertised a white trailer with a beautiful wood countertop that ran alongside the length of the trailer. When the trailer arrived, the countertop had a DECAL of a wood grain pattern stuck onto a piece of particle board! I was shocked. I immediately called to complain and asked where my wood countertop was. The gal at the other end of the phone line politely said "I'm sorry, we don't have real wood in China." *Wait! What???*

This leads me to today. A lot of people are experiencing money problems with rapidly rising inflation. If you are a conservative spender, now is not a good time to invest hard-earned capital into an unproven/new business. It's also not the time to get locked into a lease of a brick + mortar storefront. We are lucky to be living in the internet age. Through our computer or smartphone, we can sell almost anything to anyone, anywhere in the world!

My challenge this year was to seek an opportunity that anyone could do if they wanted to. My personal goal was to spotlight a niche that could serve my many friends that are looking for a side-hustle to help pay for gas and rising grocery prices. I believe I have found it in wood burning.

ARE YOU READY TO BEGIN?

Chapter 2: The Power of $20

What do you need to get started? Just $20. Yes, you read that right. The main piece of equipment you need to purchase is a basic wood burning tool.

Essential Wood Burning Tools

Wood Burners: You can find a decent plug-in wood burning tool from tool giant Harbor Freight, Hobby Lobby and Michaels Arts & Crafts stores also stock them and they are usually priced at about $15. Remember that all 3 mega stores offer weekly coupons where you can often snag 25-50% off these prices. The basic wood burning tool I use is from Walnut Hollow, it has an on/off switch and is found to be cheapest of all on Amazon ($13.67 at the time of this publishing).

Hot Tip: I carry this Walnut Hollow Woodburner Tool in my Amazon Influencer Storefront and welcome you to visit & shop at:

amazon.com/shop/tattoodirectory

All these stores sell the basic wood burning tool complete with the 3 nibs that you will need to produce just about every design. Be aware that there are more expensive wood burning kits out there ($100-$300) and although they may be more convenient (they heat up faster, etc.) you can still do ALL the techniques you need with the basic $15 wood burning tool, I promise you.

Wood: The easiest surfaces to get started on are wood slices. Amazon sells 3 ½" slices for less than $1 each. Michaels Arts & Crafts is also a good place to purchase them when using their coupons, and Hobby Lobby recently added a lot of wood craft stock at great prices. In these stores, they usually offer birch and basswood. I like the basswood since the bark/skin (live edge) on birch slices tends to fall off easier.

You can also use driftwood, wood scraps strewn around forest floors, or even cut your own! I recently purchased a hand saw from Lowes for $13 to cut my own slices from trees that have fallen in my neighborhood. The caveat with cutting your own is that the wood needs to be completely dry or the wood slices crack and split.

Dollar stores have an amazing selection of items to burn, from inexpensive wooden spoons to cutting boards to rolling pins, frames and a zillion other items!

Goodwill is another treasure shop for wood items you can embellish. Just be sure that the wood hasn't been coated with any sealing chemicals that could produce toxic fumes when burning.

Other Surfaces: You can also use your wood burning tool to create designs on leather, gourds, construction boots, cowboy hats, wood earrings and other jewelry. Lots and lots of things to wood burn!

So Many Things to Burn:

- Key Chains
- Jewelry Boxes
- Earrings
- Bangle Bracelets
- Coasters
- Ornaments
- Charcuterie Boards
- Cutting Boards
- Wooden Spoons
- Felt Hats
- Drink Flight Paddles
- Wooden Plant Marker Sticks
- **AND MUCH MORE!!!**

Additional Helpful Items For Wood Burning

-Lead Pencil/Eraser

-Small Fan (to direct fumes away from you)

-Good Lighting

-Printer/Paper for Copying & Printing Designs

 -Sealant For Finishing (*more later in book)

-Plug Power Strip

-X-acto Knife

Chapter 3: Everyone Can Do This!

"But I'm Not Creative…"

Trust me, everyone can do this! Minimalistic designs are literally the rage today. Simple designs over complex is what sells and that makes life great for the beginner wood burner! Simplistic designs can look fantastic on wood slices.

I believe that almost any adult can manage to burn a simple design onto wood. If you can draw a literal stick figure, you can do this. The only group that should not be using a wood burner tool is children, as the tool gets very hot and can cause serious burns when handled improperly. And perhaps something that could present challenges would be if you had extremely shaky hands. Steady hands make things easier, but not 100% necessary. Finger and wrist strength is not important because burning isn't achieved with pressure, just hot temperatures.

The three tips (nibs) that come standard with almost all wood burning tool kits, will allow you to create almost any effect that you want. We'll talk about them more in the next chapter.

SAFETY NOTE: It is very important to note that because this tool does get VERY hot when plugged in and turned on, it can cause harmful burns or even a house fire if left unattended. So please NEVER leave your wood burning tool turned on when you walk away from your work area. Also, keep a jug of water nearby in the event that you forget to pay attention to the wood burning tool and it catches something on fire. When I am finished with my project for that session, I not only turn the unit off, but I also unplug it, just to be super safe.

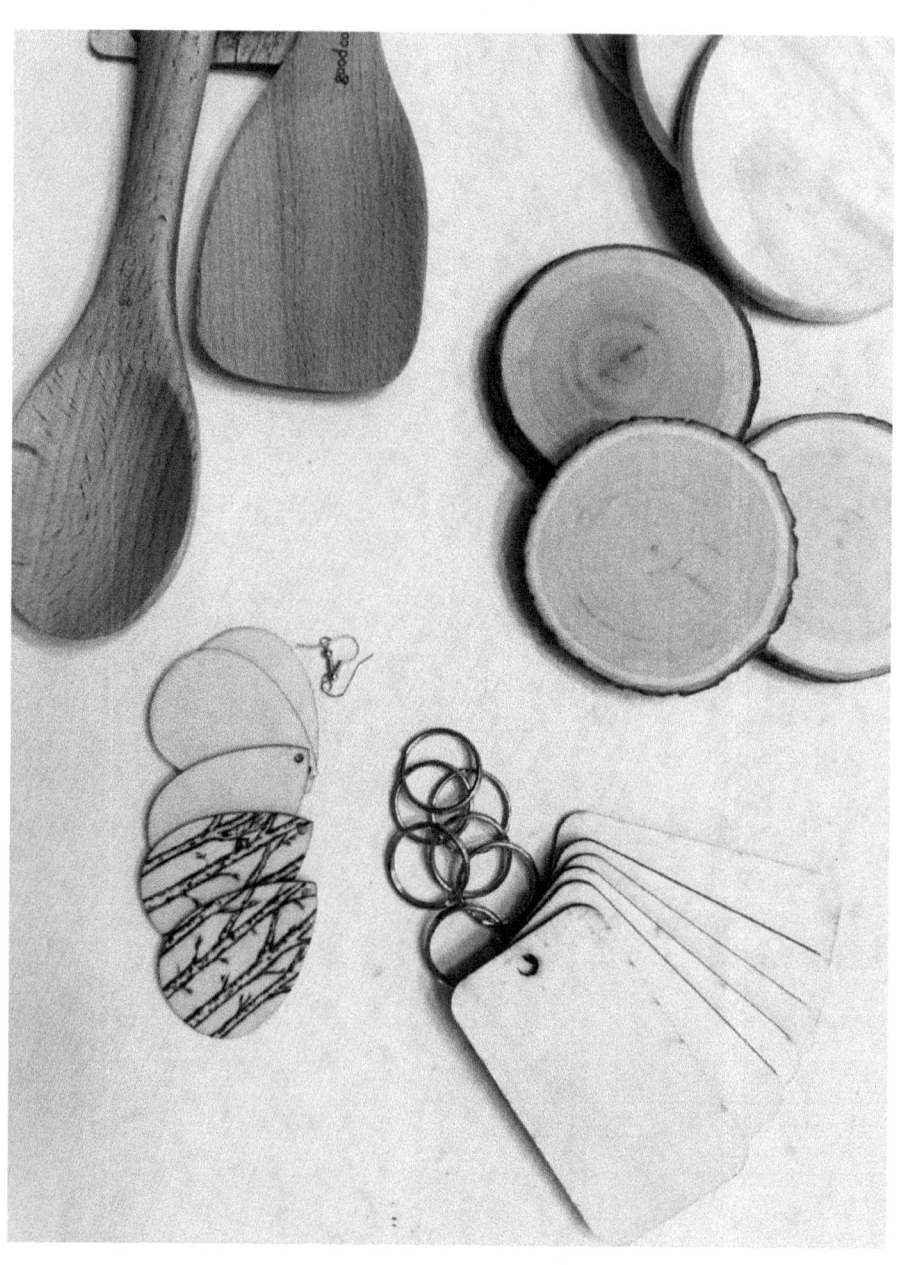

So many items to burn!

Chapter 4: Wood Burning Income 101

This book was never intended to be a complete how-to guide to the technique of wood burning, also known as "pyrography." There are so many great and in-depth books available (Amazon.com) that go into great detail about the art of wood burning and the many techniques to learn about. My mission is to teach you how to earn some extra side-hustle dollars with just basic, rudimentary wood burning skills.

We are going to keep this basic step-by-step wood burning tutorial simple and uncomplicated so you can just get going on your wood burning journey. You can successfully make some basic projects that can earn you some extra dollars without being an advanced wood burning expert.

Work Area

I like to work in a brightly lit room, whether from windows or lights. I have all the tools I will need nearby. I have a small, inexpensive desk fan that sits on my desk/work area so I can blow the wood burning fumes away from me, instead of inhaling them.

Choose Your Surface & Sand It

You can burn designs onto many different surfaces; from pre-cut wood slices to large dried gourds. Wood earrings to leather clothing. Felt cowboy hats to combat boots. Rolling pins to cutting boards. The possibilities are literally endless.

For this book we are going to reference working on wood slices. They are easy to sell, plentiful and small enough to finish in a single sitting.

Sanding - The first thing I do is lightly sand my surface with very fine sandpaper (#220 grit). This will help your wood burning nibs glide across the wood surface as opposed to getting stuck in the grooves of the wood grain. If you forget to sand the surface, that's ok, too. No big deal.

Stencilling - Most of the pieces I wood burn are executed from a stencil that I have applied to the wood. You are certainly more than welcome to pencil your design directly onto the wood, if you wish! But let's imagine you are more comfortable having a stencil to guide you. All craft stores have a large section of pre-made stencils. You can use any of them. There are literally stencils created of almost everything, so have fun shopping for your next design. I usually work from something I have found on the internet so I always have to create my own stencil.

Transferring the Stencil

Find a design you like, print it out. Now you will transfer the design onto wood. There are a few different ways to transfer your design from the paper directly onto the wood.

Method #1- Graphite Paper

You can purchase sheets of graphite paper inexpensively and use that as the transfer medium. It works by putting a graphite sheet underneath your computer paper that has the design on it (carbon side facing wood) and then trace over the top of your design. When you lift the design paper and graphite sheet you will see that the pressure from your tracing has created your stencil below directly onto the wood.

As with all tracing methods, once you start tracing, you cannot lift up and shift paper midway through. The best part about graphite paper is that you can use it over and over again. And as always, if you can't locate your own graphite paper, you can find it in my Amazon shop: *(Amazon.com/shop/tattoodirectory)*

Method #2- Pencil Stencil

This is when you reproduce the design onto the wood by essentially making your own graphite paper yourself. All you need is a pencil that has dark lead (versus soft lead). I usually prefer this method.

I rub a pencil back and forth across the back of the computer paper that the design is on. I go back and forth and back and forth until I see solid dark gray with no light spots. When the back of the paper has enough graphite on it, it will transfer nicely when you trace over the topside. Using this "by-hand" method is not only cheaper (all you need is a pencil!) but also easier for placement layout.

Both methods have advantages. I use the graphite paper method when I am doing a larger piece (anything larger than 4" diameter). But I like the by-hand method when I am doing my tiny pieces (approx. 3.5"). And because there is no graphite paper with my by-hand method, I can see where I am placing my design much easier.

There are probably even more ways to apply stencils, but between both of these methods, you will be able to transfer any design onto anything you want.

Erasing Stencil Mistakes

HOT TIP: The graphite paper stencil method isn't as easy to erase when you have created a stencil line you don't want. You may have to sand it off or scrape it away with a razor or X-Acto knife, as opposed to using a common pencil eraser. A common pencil eraser, however, will easily erase your stencil lines that were created with the hand-done pencil method.

Setting Up The Wood Burning Tool

It's time to choose the nib (tip) you want to use. Most likely you will want the writer tip. That's for outlining and creating basic lines, as if it was your pen or pencil. I recommend practicing on a "throw-away" wood scrap that is solely for your experimentation. No pressure here. Just doodle and see what it feels like holding a tool that gets hot and sometimes creates smoke puffs.

Wood burning is unique in that you can't choke down on your grip, like when you hold a pencil or paintbrush. You are forced to hold the tool a few inches away from its tip, by design, since getting your fingers too close to the tip could cause burns. As weird as it feels, I promise you that you will get used to it. All it will take is practice, practice, practice.

Letter Stamps You Can Burn With

Time To Burn Wood

The interchangeable tips of the tool are called "nibs".

There are many different style nibs but you only need

to know about these 4 at this stage of the game:

Writer tip- used to create lines like you would with a

pen or pencil.

Shader tip- allows you to gradient shade in larger

areas (but not great for solid fill)

Round filler tip- allows you to fill in areas more solidly

Skew tip- perfect for long lines and straight edges

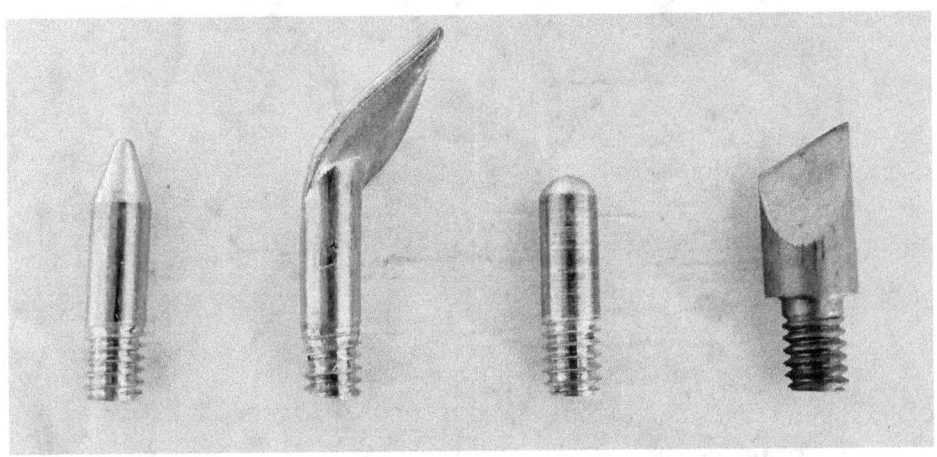

I have included several designs at the back of this book that are great starter images. The most important thing at this part is to JUST DO IT. Don't worry about the outcome. No analysis paralysis please!!!

Remember...**EVERYONE can do this!!!**

Keep a piece of experimental wood nearby. Doodle a few lines on it with your hot wood burner to get the feel and limber your hand up. Then proceed to your wood piece that has the stencil on it. Take a deep breath, exhale and start wood burning. The fun begins NOW! You will have to practice with pressure and speed of hand. The harder you press the deeper the burn, and the slower your move your tool, the darker the burn. So many different effects can be achieved here, between pressure and hand speed. This is where you will have to develop your preferred wood burned look. Some people work very very lightly, and their signature style is a very soft light brown look. It can be so attractive!

Some people work with a heavy hand and enjoy the deep burned grooves and very dark effects. Some people work in dots and enjoy creating artwork using just dots to create their intended design. Maybe you will develop your own original signature style.

There is no right or wrong here.

Here are 5 reasons why you need to try this:

1. If you make a mistake, you can scrape it off and start again.

2. Wood slices cost less than a dollar, so if you want to trash one

and start again, you can without breaking the bank.

3. Most designs on small pieces of wood can be completed

in less than 30 minutes.

4. There is not alot of competition in the wood burning market

and I find more people are amateurs than experts.

5. Everyone loves wood!!!!

Summary

-Sand surface

-Print and trace your design/stencil OR draw design by hand

-Choose your burning nib and screw it manually onto tool

-Plug in and turn wood burning tool on and let it heat up to its

maximum heat output (might take a few minutes)

-You are ready to go!

Finishing Up

By now you have wood burned a small wood slice, and I am certain it looks good! This is not the time to be a harsh critic. Pat yourself on the back! Everyone loves wood and no one will have any idea how you made your piece. Perfection is not the goal here. Burning a simple design into a wood slice is all that is needed. You are now an official pyrographic artist!

Sealing the Wood

The next step is sealing your piece. If you go on Google, you will see many different products people like to seal their wood with, from mineral oil to beeswax to varnish.

I have tried them all and find that the different options make very different outcomes! Mineral Oil and Butcher Block Conditioner leave the piece somewhat darker than when you started. They also bring out the wood's natural grain which can interfere and compete with the artwork you have added. Danish Oil is wonderful. You can purchase it online or at Lowe's/Home Depot. It doesn't darken the wood very much and is a nice pleasant oil sealer. Clear acrylic coating, polyurethane & varnish also work well and generally leave the piece as unstained as possible with a strong, waterproof acrylic seal. Great for drink coasters.

With all the various sealants, simply follow the directions on the particular product label. And of course, always use in a well-ventilated area.

As much as I wish the wood could stay untreated because of the overall wood lightness in color, it still needs to be sealed to prevent water staining, dirt marks, etc.

Chapter 5: Where To Sell

Now that you have burned some wood pieces to sell, where are you going to sell them? Here are some great ideas for you to try.

Facebook

Still the most powerful platform for the biggest reach = quick cash. Most people have Facebook accounts (I understand that Gen Z'ers, etc. don't use it as much but we will talk about their preferred platforms in a minute) so post your work. Show your friends and fam what you are doing. Post photos of you while you are actually wood burning. Show them photos of the completed piece. Let them know that you can personalize a piece for them. Tell them about your journey up to that point.

For example, let's say you are doing a simple snowflake design, let your friends and fam know that you can add their favorite person's name to it (or their pets!). Share details about your wood burning experience, people love details. People scroll FB to be entertained in one way or another, so share something about you and why you are wood burning or about your side-hustle dreams. The more authentic and heartfelt your post is, the more people will respond to it.

HOT TIP: If you have an unusually small FB following, join several local FB boards in your area. Every town in our country has zillions of friendly FB boards for you to join. Then join some FB wood burning boards and "friend" the folks there, so you will have a new network of "friends" to share your wood burning journey with.

I recently started a new FB board that I welcome you to join called *"Woodburning For Fun."* This board is so new so there aren't too many in it yet but it will grow and you're welcome to ask questions or advertise your woodcrafts for sale there. Note: sometimes "woodburning" is spelled in 2 words (woodburning) and sometimes one (wood burning).

https://www.facebook.com/groups/woodburningforfun

I'm always grateful that posting to social media is completely free. It's a marketing tool with a reach that is second to none for virtually no cost. So let's definitely utilize that!

HOT TIP: During the holidays, wood slices make for incredible Christmas tree ornaments, but after the holidays, small wood slices are just as popular for use as drink coasters. As coasters, you can sell them as a set of 4...for more money than a single ornament :)

Lisa Fasulo

Facebook Marketplace

I'm no fan of Mark Zuckerburg... but, his FB Marketplace platform is absolutely outstanding. If you have never been on FB Marketplace before, go check it out. It can be found by clicking the little house/shop icon on the FB toolbar. It's in different places on your screen depending on your device, but the shop/house symbol is always the same. Click it and explore.

You can shop solely in your local area or anywhere in the country, depending on your settings - that you can easily adjust.

Creating a listing there is dramatically easier and faster than Ebay and Etsy (very large markets in their own right). I have sold on Ebay and Etsy for years and am not going to recommend them because of their listing complexity. They are fair to good sales vehicles for the seasoned seller, but you don't need to slog through their listing procedures at this point. Also the competition is FIERCE on those 2 platforms because of their large global-wide reach.

I am a die-hard fan (for many different reasons) of FB Marketplace and I believe sales to be stronger there anyway!

Tips For a Successful Marketplace Listing:

Photos will sell the product. Shoot a lot of photos of your piece to get about 10 photos that are really clear, really attractive and well-lit. Pay attention to the backgrounds, shadows etc. Good photos are everything, I can't stress this enough. It's the difference between selling and making money and NOT. Taking good photos is too broad a skill to discuss in this booklet, so suffice it to say if you don't take good photos get a friend to do it or have them teach you.

Write a good listing title and description. Basically the more words the better. People love details to have a better understanding of what they are buying and helps them feel more comfortable about purchasing.

See an example on the next page.

Art. woodburned plaque by local artist.
$100

Send seller a message

Hi, is this available? **Send**

Alerts | Send Offer | Share | Save

(Note: This is not my listing from FB Marketplace)

My Critique

The photo is excellent but the title is not. I would write something like:

Beautiful Hand-Made 8" Wood burned Art Wood Slice

Then maybe a description like:

*I wood burned this 8" diameter basswood slice by hand with my own original design. It is signed by me on the back. (*show photo of artist signature) I sealed this piece with 3 coats of polycrylic sealer. I'd be happy to ship.*
Great gift for that wood lover we all know!

My listing would have 6-8 photos showing the piece well and with different backgrounds and angles. Before your listing goes live, FB Marketplace will ask you a few things. One, if you want only local buyers, which would come in person (or you meet them somewhere) and pay you directly or secondly, if you would consider shipping your item. I like to click that option because I find it easy to navigate the FB Marketplace process regarding shipping etc. But for your initial sales, let's keep it local, so you can get comfortable with the FB sales process.

Next, it will ask you if you want this listing to be seen on your personal FB page or on other online FB boards that you belong to. I always decline that option and only list on Marketplace, but that option is totally up to you!

I have enjoyed tremendous success from selling on FB Marketplace over the years and I have noticed a rather strange by-product: the incredibly wonderful people I have met on there! I don't know actually why that is, but the people I have bought from and sold to have been 100% memorably sweet. And because Marketplace is through FB, you are able to spy on their profile page to see what the person is like that you are selling to.

I'm going to rate this sales platform an A+.

Other Places to Sell Your Pieces

Craigslist: don't do it.

Too many scammers and creepy people on there. It was a decent platform a long, long, long time ago but don't waste your time there now.

Instagram: easy and strong as well.

For many, it's more powerful than FB, but it depends where you are comfortable and where you have the largest following.

Pinterest: if you are social media savvy, you will already know this platform's strong sneaky reach.

The SEO on Pinterest is amazing, but if you don't know what I mean by that, don't worry, it's not necessary for you to sell your goods here for extra side-hustle money.

TikTok: if your following is young in age and comes from Gen Z and some millennials, this is a required platform to advertise your goods for sale.

This younger age group is not on FB, but they are here in droves! Also, consider opening a TikTok shop on that platform.

EBay & Etsy: too complicated for beginners.

My suggestion is to work up to listing on these platforms.

Michael's Maker Place: new & untested.

This could be a viable platform for selling your wood wares but it is too new for me to evaluate. Check it out.

These are the main online platforms I use for selling, although there are even more, these are the only ones you initially need to concern yourself with. If you have an aversion to social media in general, stick to FB/FB Marketplace.

PARTY
TIME

Wood Burning Parties

This is a GREAT vehicle for extra steady income! The only caveat here is that you need to have supplies on hand for your participants. Typically parties like this charge $35-50 per/person to reserve their space in your wood burning party. Common and manageable size groups:

6-12 people. Because of the intensely hot tool, I limit my participants to adults only.

I really enjoy hosting wood burning parties because they are a lot of FUN! Wood burning parties are easy to set up for and there isn't any clean up afterwards!

When I have wood burning parties, I include 2 wood coasters for each participant or 1 cutting board (for a greater participation fee). Then I supply them with a wood burning tool (pre-set with the writing nib) to use while they are at my party (I retain the tool, they do not get to keep that) and they can use my available stencils.

HOT TIP: most of the time, someone in your party group will then schedule and host the next party that they will want you at. Make sure to have business cards on hand to pass out so people know how to contact you easily.

Future Income Ideas From Parties:

Kits: you could always package a kit for your burners to purchase which includes a wood burning tool, different wood slices, your stencils, etc. and anything else you might want to add to entice them to purchase your kit. Remember to have a profit added to your kit item costs so this is an additional income stream for you.

Merch: maybe you want to offer your wood burning party participants T-Shirts with a clever wood burning slogan, coffee mugs or any other trendy items with your branding on it.

CraftShows/FleaMarkets/FarmersMarkets: I have sold crafts at craft shows for literally decades but that was before FREE social media. In-person shows are great for customer feedback because you will be standing there to hear what the general public has to say about your crafts. Invaluable market research and often so motivating!

Participating in crafts shows costs an entry fee, but many do offer an option of a free booth if you will demonstrate your craft but you have to ask for this option, because show organizers don't always advertise this opportunity.

Wood burning is a great craft to demonstrate because you don't need any of the many items a painter needs, such as water, etc. All you basically need is electricity.

This piece was done by a first-time burner at my first wood burning party

Chapter 6: Think Big

The only thing standing between you and a profitable wood burning business is believing that you can do it. With 4.95 billion people worldwide that use social media EVERY SINGLE DAY, there are undoubtedly customers online, waiting for your handmade art. It's up to you to get your products in front of them... or well, in front of their screens.

Here are some of my final tips for kickstarting the most successful wood burning business possible.

Pricing

This is where you can get creative. Be bold. Not many people do wood burned art so......you can charge whatever your audience will pay. I have seen prices set way too low and some that are set super high, so there is a big expanse for you and your wood burned creations somewhere in between.

It's easy to find ornaments and coasters on Etsy for too cheap (like $8-$14) and it's just as easy to find pieces on Ebay for $5000 dollars and upwards (sounds like alot to me but hey....way to go!). The easiest way to price your work is to keep track of the hours you have put into your piece, and stick to that. You know what you need to earn per hour to make this worth your time.

I don't do anything for less than $25/hr but $50 is my more common per hour fee and I aspire to a flat $100 per hour. Don't worry what others are charging for a similar size piece of wood, etc. instead: do YOU.

Here's a story that may help you see that sometimes people equate price with quality; the higher price, the better it must be. We know this isn't always true but it's often a common shopper perception.

Price Perception Matters

Here goes. Another side hustle I have had for the last several years is custom miniature pet portraits on tiny canvas. I started by charging $20 because I was learning the craft and knew that they weren't coming out that great at the time.

Then, with a lot of practice, I became more proficient so I raised my prices to $35. They sold well. After even more practice I raised my prices to $48. They still sold steadily.

After hand painting hundreds of mini pet portraits, I was getting tired and wanted to cut back on orders. So I raised my prices to $75 thinking the orders would slow to a crawl which is what I secretly hoped for. But guess what? They haven't slowed at all, and maybe even orders have increased! All this tells me is that I never charged enough!!!! I never priced them accurately for the last several years!!!! UGH! So the moral of this story is be sure and charge enough money when you feel satisfied with your level of proficiency.

Giving Away Pieces for Free?

Another marketing element I often use when I'm learning a new craft, is to give some pieces away FOR FREE. Especially to people who I know will show them to friends and re-post on their own social media accounts. It's a great way to get your name out there.

it didn't cost me anything other than the piece of wood I worked on and the publicity I got from that will most definitely pay off, it always does. I also donate a few pieces a year to a school, veteran or animal-based charity that hosts a large yearly auction. Great advertising opportunities!

Remember that your new skill doesn't have to be always done on wood. The latest craze right now is burned felt cowboy hats (VERY expensive hats). They are super pretty and prices run deep into the hundreds. There's many videos on YouTube.com showing you how to do them. Easy and fun!

There's also "fractal burning," look it up on YouTube.com, looks kind of scary to me but super beautiful effects can be created from that.

Another huge wood burning opportunity worth talking about are the laser/engraving machines. You can find them on Amazon.com (and in my Amazon Influencer Store) as well as Michaels Arts & Crafts, but the pricing varies greatly per machine brand. Prices can range from $300 into the thousands. How these work is that you program the machine (via your computer) to burn (or engrave) your design for you.

The final product is super solid and professional and the detail that can be achieved is outstanding. Great for mass producing items for larger markets. Check it out and always keep on the lookout for the next big wood burning trend.

The cat key chain design above was created by a Glowforge machine. I don't personally own a machine like this as I prefer to work by hand but the potential for mass-produced items is VERY enticing!

welcome

Welcome

hello

LOL!

About the Author

Elisa Fasulo is an artist + entrepreneur. She has made a living from her arts and crafts for several decades. Whether she is painting tiny pet portraits or wood burning large live-edge wood pieces, she always keeps her eye on the latest trends & side hustles that fuel her passions and help others succeed.

www.ingramcontent.com/pod-product-compliance
Lightning Source LLC
Chambersburg PA
CBHW071158290526
45796CB00007B/71